D0907046

States
NEW YORK

by Tyler Maine

CAPSTONE PRESS
a capstone imprint

Next Page Books are published by Capstone Press,
1710 Roe Crest Drive, North Mankato, Minnesota 56003
www.mycapstone.com

Library of Congress Cataloging-in-Publication Data
Cataloging-in-publication information is on file with the Library of
Congress.
ISBN 978-1-5157-0419-5 (library binding)
ISBN 978-1-5157-0478-2 (paperback)
ISBN 978-1-5157-0530-7 (ebook PDF)

Editorial Credits
Jaclyn Jaycox, editor; Kazuko Collins and Katy LaVigne, designers;
Morgan Walters, media researcher; Tori Abraham, production specialist

Photo Credits
Capstone Press: Angi Gahler, map 4, 7; Corbis: Bettmann, middle 19,
bottom 19, Courtesy of Glyndebourne Festival Opera; Ira Nowinski, top
19; Getty Images: Photographer's Choice/Lisa J. Goodman, top left 20,
Science Faction/Library of Congress, top 18, Stocktrek Images/John
Parrot, middle 18, Stone/John Kuczala, bottom right 20; iStockphoto:
EdStock, 14; Library of Congress: H. O'Neil, 31 Union Square, New
York, 27, Prints and Photographs Division, 12, 28; One Mile Up,
Inc., flag, seal 23; Shutterstock: Al Mueller, bottom left 20, Andrea J
Smith, middle left 21, Andrew Hagen, top 24, Andrey Bayda, 17, Bruce
MacQueen, middle right 21, ChameleonsEye, 29, CristinaMuraca, 10,
Debby Wong, bottom 24, Doug Lemke, 7, Everett Historical, 25, 26,
Filip Fuxa, top right 21, Frank L Junior, top right 20, IM_photo, cover,
5, Imfoto, top left 21, jiawangkun, 13, John A. Anderson, bottom left
8, Johnathan Esper, 11, littleny, 16, Osugi, 15, R Rusak, 9, Rene Pi,
6, s_bukley, bottom 18, Stuart Monk, bottom right 8, Timolina, bottom
right 21, Yellowj, bottom left 21

All design elements by Shutterstock

Printed and bound in China.
0316/CA21600187
012016   009436F16

TABLE OF CONTENTS

Want to take your research further? Ask your librarian if your school subscribes to PebbleGo Next. If so, when you see this helpful symbol ⓚ throughout the book, log onto www.pebblegonext.com for bonus downloads and information.

LOCATION

New York is located in the northeastern United States. Canada and Lake Ontario lie to the north. To the south are New Jersey and Pennsylvania. Vermont, Massachusetts, and Connecticut run along New York's eastern edge. New York's southeast corner faces the Atlantic Ocean. Lake Erie and Canada are on the west. New York's capital, Albany, is on the Hudson River. New York City, Buffalo, and Rochester are the state's biggest cities.

PebbleGo Next Bonus!
To print and label your own map, go to www.pebblegonext.com and search keywords:

NY MAP

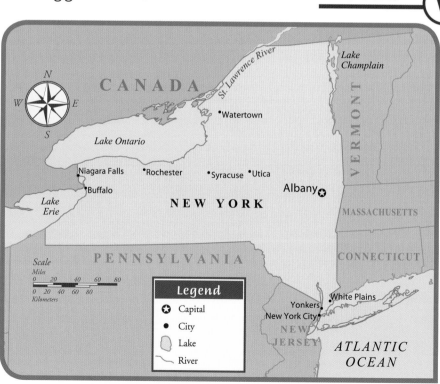

New York City is the largest city in the United States.

GEOGRAPHY

New York has mountains, rivers, and lakes. The Appalachian Mountains cover the state's eastern half. Within this area are the Finger Lakes. These 11 lakes are long and thin, like fingers. Rivers flow through this area. The Hudson River runs down eastern New York. It flows into the Atlantic Ocean at New York City. The Adirondack Mountains are in northern New York. The state's highest point, Mount Marcy, is in the Adirondacks. It reaches a peak of 5,344 feet (1,629 meters).

PebbleGo Next Bonus!
To watch a video about Niagara Falls, go to www.pebblegonext.com and search keywords:

NY VIDEO

New York has 127 miles (204 kilometers) of coastline along the Atlantic Ocean.

A large sheet of ice passing through New York thousands of years ago is resposible for most of the state's natural features.

St. Lawrence River

Lake Champlain

ADIRONDACK MOUNTAINS

▲ Mount Marcy

Lake Ontario

Oneida Lake

Mohawk River

APPALACHIAN REGION

Niagara Falls

CENTRAL LOWLAND

Finger Lakes

Susquehanna River

Lake Erie

Genesee River

CATSKILL MOUNTAINS

Hudson River

Legend

▲	Highest Point
🔷	Lake
⛰	Mountain Range
○	Point of Interest
〜	River

Delaware River

Long Island Sound

COASTAL PLAIN

Long Island

Scale
Miles
0   20   40   60   80
0   20   40   60   80
Kilometers

ATLANTIC OCEAN

WEATHER

New York has cool winters and warm summers. The average January temperature is 21 degrees Fahrenheit (minus 6 degrees Celsius). The average July temperature is 69°F (21°C).

Average High and Low Temperatures (New York, NY)

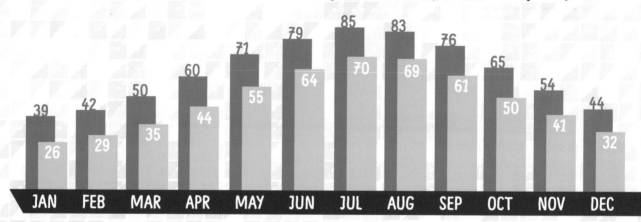

JAN	FEB	MAR	APR	MAY	JUN	JUL	AUG	SEP	OCT	NOV	DEC
39	42	50	60	71	79	85	83	76	65	54	44
26	29	35	44	55	64	70	69	61	50	41	32

Niagara Falls

Every minute at Niagara Falls, millions of gallons of rushing water cascade over a 180-foot (55-m) drop. This natural wonder crosses the border between New York and Canada.

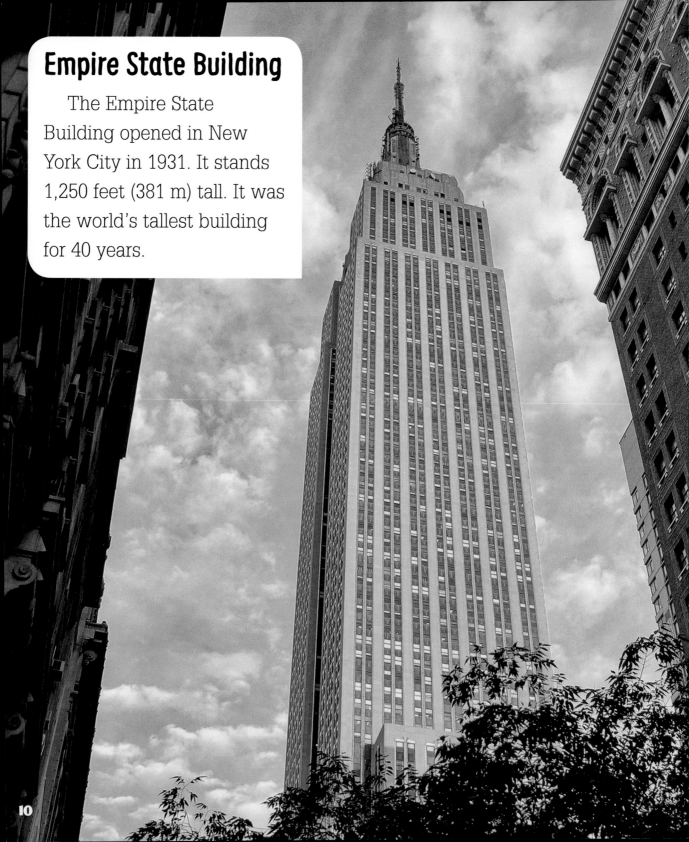

Empire State Building

The Empire State Building opened in New York City in 1931. It stands 1,250 feet (381 m) tall. It was the world's tallest building for 40 years.

Adirondack Park

This huge wilderness area is larger than Yellowstone, Yosemite, Grand Canyon, Glacier, and Great Smokies National Parks combined. The park covers 6 million acres (2.4 million hectares) and has 3,000 lakes and ponds.

British General John Burgoyne surrenders to American General Horatio Gates after the Battle of Saratoga.

In 1609 Henry Hudson left the Netherlands and sailed into what is now the Hudson River. Dutch settlers followed and founded the colony of New Netherlands in 1624. Other Dutch settlers set up New Amsterdam in 1625. The British took over New Netherlands in 1664 and changed its name to New York. New Amsterdam became today's New York City.

New Yorkers joined the other American colonists in the Revolutionary War (1775–1783). The colonists won their freedom from Great Britain in 1783. New York became the 11th U.S. state in 1788.

New York's state government has three branches. The governor heads the executive branch. The legislature is made up of the Senate with 61 members and the Assembly with 150 members. They make the laws for New York. The judicial branch upholds the laws.

It took more than 25 years to build New York's state capitol building. It was completed in 1899.

INDUSTRY

New York's natural resources help make it a leader in manufacturing and agriculture. The state has plenty of water for homes, factories, and farms. The state's waters are also used to transport goods. Factories in New York City produce clothing, office equipment, books, and magazines.

The New York Stock Exchange is the largest stock exchange in the world.

New York is one of the world's biggest business and communication centers. New York City is an international banking center and home to the New York Stock Exchange. New York City also is the publishing capital of the United States. Hundreds of publishers and several large newspapers are located there.

The *New York Times* newspaper was founded in 1851.

POPULATION

Immigrants from many lands entered the country through Ellis Island in New York Harbor. Many immigrants from Italy, Ireland, Great Britain, and other nations remained in New York. More than 3 million New Yorkers have roots in Spanish-speaking countries such as Puerto Rico, Mexico, and Cuba. Almost 3 million African-Americans live in New York. Another 1.4 million New Yorkers are Asians. They came from China, India, Korea, the Philippines, and Japan.

Population by Ethnicity

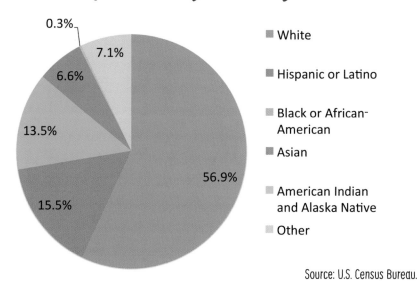

- 0.3%
- 7.1%
- 6.6%
- 13.5%
- 15.5%
- 56.9%

- White
- Hispanic or Latino
- Black or African-American
- Asian
- American Indian and Alaska Native
- Other

Source: U.S. Census Bureau.

FAMOUS PEOPLE

Franklin Delano Roosevelt (1882–1945) was the 32nd president of the United States (1933–1945). He was born in Hyde Park.

Theodore Roosevelt (1858–1919) was the 26th president of the United States (1901–1909). He was born in New York City.

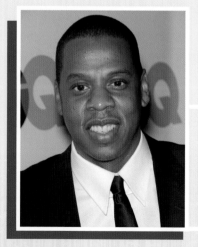

Jay-Z (Sean Corey Carter) (1969–) is a Grammy Award–winning rapper, record producer, film producer, and businessman. He was born in Brooklyn.

Maurice Sendak (1928–2012) wrote and illustrated award-winning children's books, including *Where the Wild Things Are*. He was born in New York City.

Sojourner Truth (1797–1883) was a powerful speaker against slavery and for women's rights. Her real name was Isabella Baumfree. She was born a slave near Kingston.

Frederic Remington (1861–1909) made paintings and sculptures of cowboys and horses. He was born in Canton.

STATE SYMBOLS

Tree

sugar maple

Flower

rose

Bird

bluebird

Fish

brook trout

PebbleGo Next Bonus! To make New York's state muffin, go to www.pebblegonext.com and search keywords: NY RECIPE

Gemstone

garnet

Fruit

apple

Reptile

snapping turtle

Animal

beaver

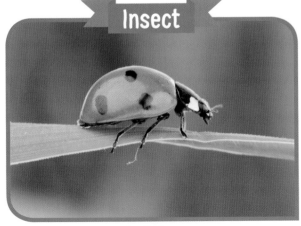

Insect

ladybug

Muffin

apple muffin

21

FAST FACTS

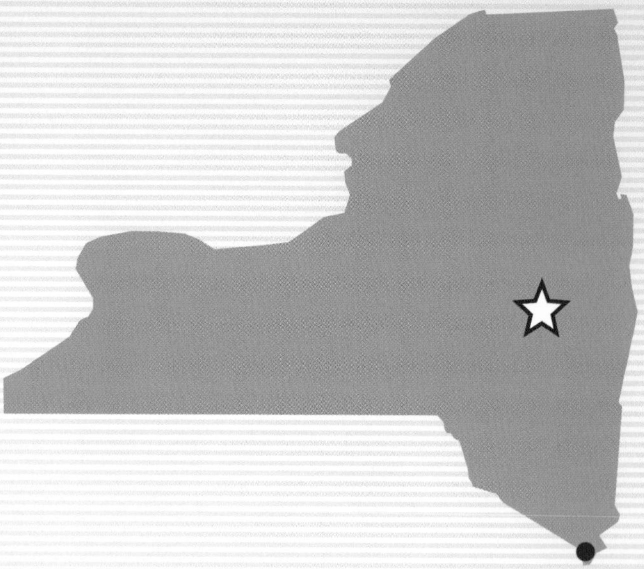

STATEHOOD
1788

CAPITAL ☆
Albany

LARGEST CITY ●
New York City

SIZE
47,126 square miles (122,056 square kilometers) land area
(2010 U.S. Census Bureau)

POPULATION
19,651,127 (2013 U.S. Census estimate)

STATE NICKNAME
The Empire State

STATE MOTTO
"Excelsior," which is Latin for "ever upward"

STATE SEAL

The Great Seal of New York includes the State Coat of Arms. The coat of arms shows Liberty and Justice standing beside a shield. At Liberty's feet is a crown to show the state's freedom from Great Britain. Justice holds a sword and a scale. These symbols represent the fairness needed in government. The shield has a picture of the sun rising behind a mountain range. Boats cross the Hudson River to show trade. Above the shield is a bald eagle. Below the shield is a banner with the state motto, "Excelsior."

PebbleGo Next Bonus!
To print and color your own flag, go to www.pebblegonext.com and search keywords:
NY FLAG

STATE FLAG

The New York flag was adopted in 1778. The flag is dark blue with the State Coat of Arms in the center. The coat of arms shows Liberty and Justice standing beside a shield. At Liberty's feet is a crown to show the state's freedom from Great Britain. Justice holds a sword and a scale. These symbols represent the fairness needed in government. The shield has a picture of the sun rising behind a mountain range. Boats cross the Hudson River to show trade. Above the shield is a bald eagle. Below the shield is a banner with the state motto, "Excelsior."

MINING PRODUCTS

salt, sand and gravel, limestone

MANUFACTURED GOODS

chemicals, computer and electronic equipment, food products, machinery, clothing, printed material

FARM PRODUCTS

apples, grapes, vegetables

PebbleGo Next Bonus! To learn the lyrics to the state song, go to www.pebblegonext.com and search keywords:

NY SONG

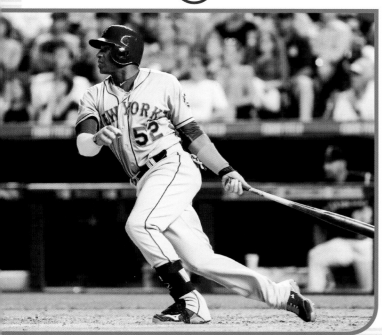

PROFESSIONAL SPORTS TEAMS

New York Mets (MLB)

New York Yankees (MLB)

New York Red Bulls (MLS)

Brooklyn Nets (NBA)

New York Knicks (NBA)

New York Liberty (WNBA)

Buffalo Bills (NFL)

New York Giants (NFL)

New York Jets (NFL)

Buffalo Sabres (NHL)

New York Islanders (NHL)

New York Rangers (NHL)

NEW YORK TIMELINE

1000
By this time Algonquin and Iroquois Indians are living in the New York area.

CIRCA 1570
The Mohawk, Oneida, Onondaga, Cayuga, and Seneca form the Iroquois Confederacy, or Five Nations.

1609
Henry Hudson explores the region for the Dutch.

1620
The Pilgrims establish a colony in the New World in present-day Massachusetts.

1624 New Netherlands colony is founded.

1664 The British conquer the area and rename it New York.

1788 On July 26 New York becomes the 11th state.

1825 Erie Canal opens.

1861–1865	The Union and the Confederacy fight the Civil War. New York fights on the Union side.
1892	Ellis Island opens in New York Harbor. It becomes a main entrance for immigrants to the United States.
1896	President Grover Cleveland dedicates the Statue of Liberty.

| 1914–1918 | World War I is fought; the United States enters the war in 1917. |

1929
Governor Franklin Delano Roosevelt starts New Deal programs to help New Yorkers.

1939–1945
World War II is fought; the United States enters the war in 1941.

1952
New York City becomes the permanent home of the United Nations.

1977 The "I Love New York" tourism campaign is created to boost tourism and help New York's economy during a recession.

2001 On September 11 terrorists attack the World Trade Center and the Pentagon.

2012 Hurricane Sandy hits the Atlantic coast on October 29. It causes widespread damage and power outages in New York and becomes the second-costliest hurricane in U.S. history.

2015 New York City is shut down by a blizzard that affects up to 60 million people in the northeast.

Glossary

executive *(ig-ZE-kyuh-tiv)*—the branch of government that makes sure laws are followed

immigrant *(IM-uh-gruhnt)*—someone who comes from abroad to live permanently in a country

industry *(IN-duh-stree)*—a business which produces a product or provides a service

international *(in-tur-NASH-uh-nuhl)*—including more than one nation

judicial *(joo-DISH-uhl)*—to do with the branch of government that explains and interprets the laws

legislature *(LEJ-iss-lay-chur)*—a group of elected officials who have the power to make or change laws for a country or state

natural resource *(NACH-ur-uhl REE-sorss)*—something in nature that people use, such as coal and trees

recession *(REE-sess-shuhn)*—temporary slowing of business activity

tourism *(TOOR-i-zuhm)*—the business of taking care of visitors to a country or place

transport *(transs-PORT)*—to move or carry something or someone from one place to another

Read More

Elish, Dan. *New York: The Empire State.* It's My State! New York: Cavendish Square Publishing, 2015.

Ganeri, Anita. *United States of America: A Benjamin Blog and His Inquisitive Dog Guide.* Country Guides. Chicago: Heinemann Raintree Library, 2015.

Malaspina, Ann. *What's Great About New York?* Our Great States. Minneapolis: Lerner Publications Company, 2015.

Internet Sites

FactHound offers a safe, fun way to find Internet sites related to this book. All of the sites on FactHound have been researched by our staff.

Here's all you do:

Visit *www.facthound.com*

Type in this code: 9781515704195

Check out projects, games and lots more at
www.capstonekids.com

Critical Thinking Using the Common Core

1. How big is Adirondack Park? (Key Ideas and Details)

2. Ellis Island opened in 1892 in New York Harbor. It became a main entrance for immigrants to the United States. What is an immigrant? (Craft and Structure)

3. What are New York's waters used for? (Key Ideas and Details)

Index